Let's Get Mapping!
Mapping Information

Melanie Waldron

Chicago, Illinois

Edited by Nancy Dickmann and Abby Colich
Designed by Victoria Allen
Original illustrations © 2013
Illustrated by HL Studios
Picture research by Ruth Blair
Originated by Capstone Global Library Limited

**Library of Congress Cataloging-in-Publication
Data**
Waldron, Melanie.
  Mapping information / Melanie Waldron.
     p. cm.—(Let's get mapping!)
  Includes bibliographical references and index.
  ISBN 9781410999313 (pb) 1. Maps—Juvenile
literature. I. Title.
  GA105.6.W345 2013
  526—dc23   2012008508

Acknowledgments
We would like to thank the following for
permission to reproduce photographs: Alamy:
Andrew Aitchison, 9, Mim Friday, 25, Robert
Matton AB, cover bottom, SFM Stock 2, 20; Flickr:
© Copyright SASI Group (University of Sheffield),
24; Shutterstock: Alleksander, 11 bottom,
gemphotography, 15, Ilike, cover top, Pincasso,
21, sirikorn thamniyom, 26, Tarasenko Sergey, 17,
Thomas La Mela, 4, Tom Grundy, 5; SuperStock:
Easy-Pix, 22, Ron Nickel/Design Pics, 23; USGS: 27

Design Elements
Shutterstock: AlexanderZam, Callahan,
HomeStudio, Laralova, LyudmilaKa, musicman,
Natykach Nataliia, nicemonkey

Every effort has been made to contact
copyright holders of any material reproduced
in this book. Any omissions will be rectified
in subsequent printings if notice is given to
the publisher.

All the Internet addresses (URLs) given in this
book were valid at the time of going to press.
However, due to the dynamic nature of the
Internet, some addresses may have changed,
or sites may have changed or ceased to exist
since publication. While the author and
publisher regret any inconvenience this may
cause readers, no responsibility for any such
changes can be accepted by either the author
or the publisher.

Contents

Some words appear in the text in bold, **like this**. You can find out what they mean by looking in the glossary.

What Is a Map?

There are lots of different types of maps. Most maps are flat pieces of paper showing information about the land. They might show the buildings and roads on the land. They might show the land's **natural features**, such as hills, mountains, and rivers. They might show other kinds of information, such as the number of people living in an area.

Some parts of the world have huge numbers of people living there. Maps can show where these places are.

Mapping different information

Many maps are really useful for showing how places are different. For example, a map could show the **percentage** of people who can read in a country. You could simply write the number on the map. But you could also use different colors, or **symbols**, to represent different numbers. If you did this for all the countries in the world, you would quickly see some patterns.

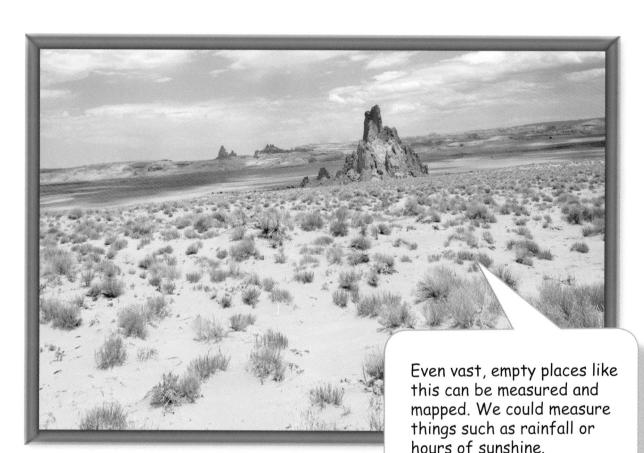

Even vast, empty places like this can be measured and mapped. We could measure things such as rainfall or hours of sunshine.

STATISTICAL MAPS

Statistics are simply amounts or numbers of something. For example, the number of tourists visiting a town is a statistic. Maps that show statistics are called statistical maps, or thematic maps.

Changing Colors

Some mapmakers use color to show information about areas on a map. The information can be split into groups, and a different shade of color is used for each group. Each area is then colored in the correct shade. A **key** can explain what each shade of color means.

The map below shows information about the time taken for children to travel to school. Areas where average journeys are short (less than five minutes) are shown in blue. Areas where journeys are very long (over 15 minutes) are shown in orange. Areas with journey times in between are shown in different shades of color.

Average journey time to school

Over 15 minutes   5–10 minutes
10–15 minutes   0–5 minutes

Use the key to figure out which areas have the longest journeys to school.

Many colors, many shades

Most colored maps use different shades of one color to show different amounts of something. This can help us to pick out patterns in the information. Sometimes darker or lighter shades of one color will be used to show more or less of something. See the map below for an example of this.

Average journey time to school

Key
- Over 15 minutes
- 10–15 minutes
- 5–10 minutes
- 0–5 minutes

Compare this map with the one on page 6. It is showing the same information, but using different colors. Which map do you think is easiest to understand?

Different Scales

Maps shrink the land down to fit in a small area. This is called scaling down. Maps that shrink things down a lot, such as country maps, are called small-scale maps. They show a large area, but there is not much detail. Small-scale maps can show information and patterns about large areas. For example, a world map of average temperatures would show that the coldest areas are near the **North Pole** and **South Pole**.

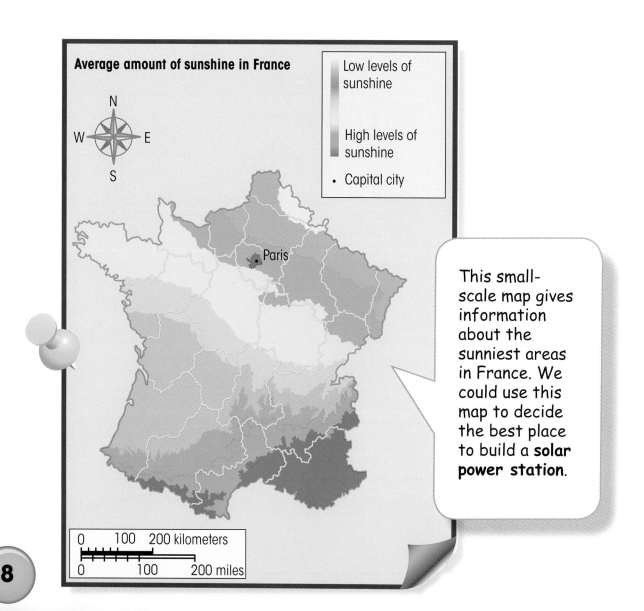

Average amount of sunshine in France

N
W E
S

Low levels of sunshine

High levels of sunshine

• Capital city

• Paris

0   100   200 kilometers
0   100   200 miles

This small-scale map gives information about the sunniest areas in France. We could use this map to decide the best place to build a **solar power station**.

Large-scale maps

Maps that shrink everything down a lot less, such as town maps, are called large-scale maps. They do not show large areas, but they can show huge amounts of detail about the land. Maps of buildings, such as hospitals or schools, are very large-scale maps. They can show very detailed information about the building—for example, where the restrooms are.

A very large-scale map of this school could show people where to find the classroom they want to visit.

Symbols on Maps

Most maps use symbols to show information about places. Symbols are usually little pictures or shapes that represent something. For example, a red cross might represent a hospital. Symbols are helpful for showing information on a map without using words.

The symbols on this map show where each type of natural **resource** can be found.

KEY

- Coal
- Gold
- Diamonds
- Oil
- Fishing

SOUTH AFRICA

INDIAN OCEAN

ATLANTIC OCEAN

North
West — East
South

FINDING KEYS

Maps that use symbols usually also have a key. A key is a list of the symbols on the map. The key explains what each symbol means. When you look at a map with symbols on it, you should always look at the key, so you understand what the map is showing you.

Bigger symbols

Symbols can be used on maps to show different amounts of things. Bigger symbols, or more symbols, mean a larger amount of something. This means that symbols show not only where something is, but also how much is there.

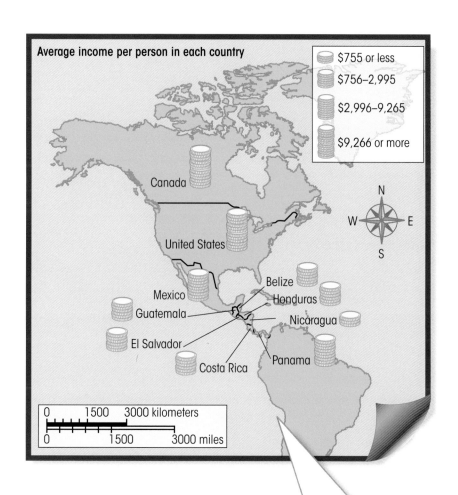

Average income per person in each country

$755 or less
$756–2,995
$2,996–9,265
$9,266 or more

Canada
United States
Mexico
Guatemala
El Salvador
Costa Rica
Belize
Honduras
Nicaragua
Panama

N W E S

0   1500   3000 kilometers
0   1500   3000 miles

This map of North America shows the average amount that people earn in a year. Tall stacks of coins show wealthy countries, and short stacks of coins show less wealthy countries.

Dot Maps

Some maps can show where there are groups, or clusters, of things. Mapmakers sometimes use little dots on maps to represent something or even a large number of things. These are called dot maps. They are very useful for locating large clusters of something.

For example, you could mark a dot for every tree you see in your neighborhood. If there is a local park with lots of trees, there would be lots of dots there. Your map would show where the clusters of trees are.

In this map of Australia, a dot represents 500 people. You can use this map to see where the heavily populated areas are.

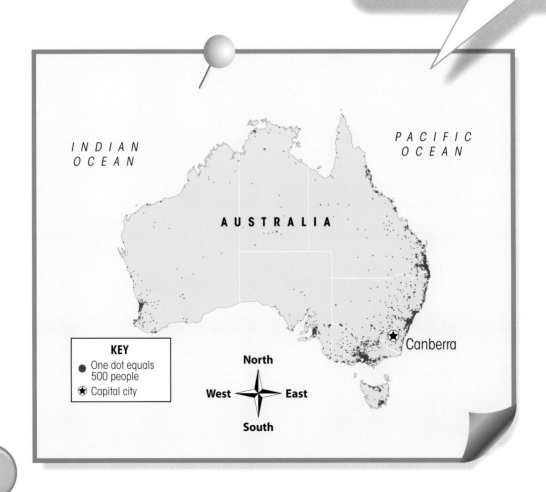

INDIAN OCEAN

PACIFIC OCEAN

AUSTRALIA

★ Canberra

KEY
● One dot equals 500 people
★ Capital city

North

West ← → East

South

Lots of dots!

Different colored dots can be used to show different groups of things. For example, if you wanted to make a map of where different animals are found in a nature reserve, you could use a different color for each type of animal. A lion could be a red dot, an elephant could be a blue dot, and so on. The map would then show clusters of animals across the reserve.

Use the key to figure out which types of animal are found across the nature reserve.

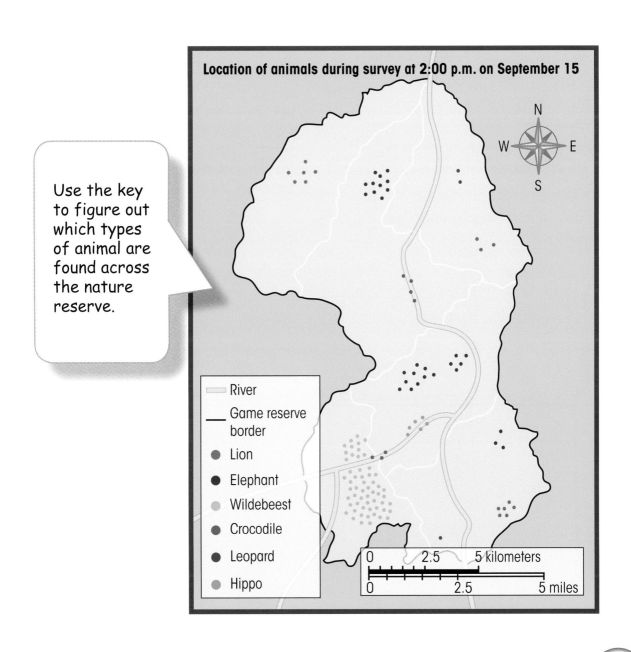

Location of animals during survey at 2:00 p.m. on September 15

River
Game reserve border
Lion
Elephant
Wildebeest
Crocodile
Leopard
Hippo

0   2.5   5 kilometers
0   2.5   5 miles

Maps Showing Movement

It is sometimes useful to show the movement of something on a map. You may have seen maps that show the movements of **ocean currents** or winds. But we can also show the movement of things such as goods or tourists.

Some maps use **flow lines** to represent the movement of something. Flow lines show where something comes from and goes to. If we wanted to show different amounts, we could use thicker or thinner flow lines to represent these amounts.

This flow line map shows that far more people travel to work from towns to the city. This is shown by a thicker flow line.

Traffic flow between 7:00 a.m. and 10:00 a.m.

Town

City

Built-up area   → Traffic flow

Countryside

Lots of people travel to work in one direction, and very few travel in the other direction. Flow line maps can show us this kind of information.

All directions

Flow lines do not have to go in just two directions, forward and backward. They can go in all directions to show all the places that something moves to. For example, a map of your country could show flow lines for its exports (items sold to other countries). A flow line would go from your country to every country that receives exports. The flow lines could be different thicknesses to show that more exports go to some countries.

Maps About History

Maps are not only useful for learning about today. They also help us to understand the past. Lots of historical information can be shown on a map. For example, maps can show the routes that explorers took across oceans and countries. Maps can also show us where historical battles were won and lost.

This map shows Lewis and Clark's route as they explored the western part of North America in 1804–1806.

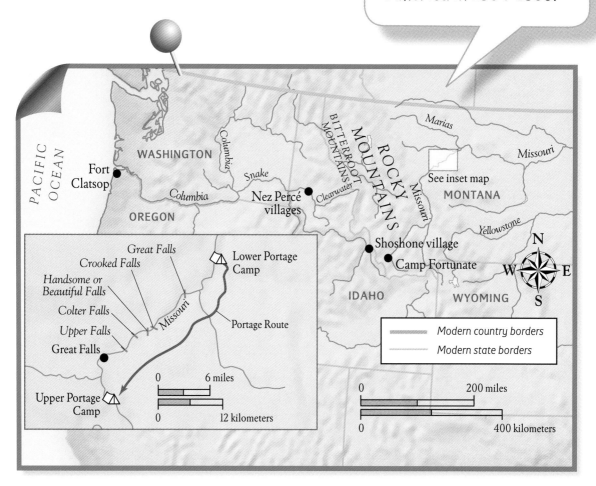

Maps from the past

People have been making maps for hundreds of years. We know that today's maps are very accurate because we can use **satellite images** and **aerial photographs** to check them. In the past, people simply had to draw maps using sketches of the land.

Some really old maps look very different from today's maps. They were made when people did not know about all of the world. Lots of world maps made by the Romans do not show North America or South America, because they did not know these lands existed.

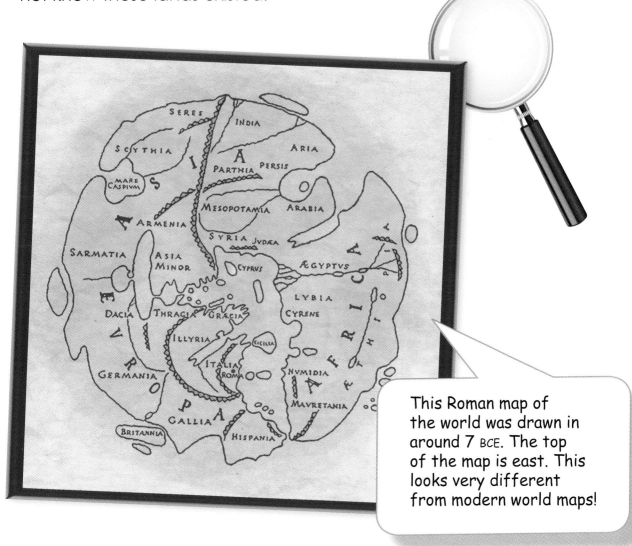

This Roman map of the world was drawn in around 7 BCE. The top of the map is east. This looks very different from modern world maps!

Equal Lines and Time Zones

It is sometimes useful to see where things are the same on a map. Where lots of places have the same amount of something, such as rainfall, we can connect these points with lines. Lines that join equal points are called **isolines**.

For example, you could mark distance isolines on a map of your school and the local area. You could draw a circle on the map to show everything that is half a mile (0.8 kilometer) from your school. You could then draw more circles, at 1 mile (1.6 kilometers), 1.5 miles (2.4 kilometers), 2 miles (3.2 kilometers), and so on.

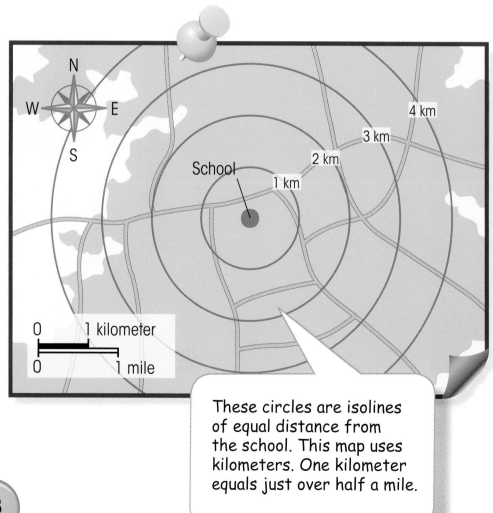

These circles are isolines of equal distance from the school. This map uses kilometers. One kilometer equals just over half a mile.

Time zones

Across the world, the time of day is different. World maps can show all the different time zones on a map. These are areas where the time is the same. You can use a time-zone map to figure out what the time will be in another country.

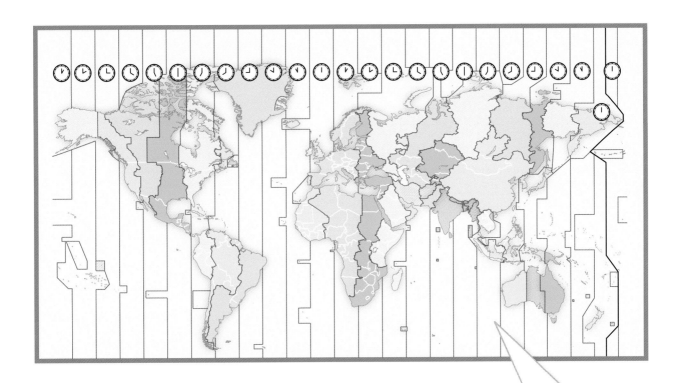

MANY TIME ZONES

Some time-zone lines are "bent" to follow a country's **border**, so that the time is the same across the country. Large countries, such as the United States, need to have several time zones.

Moving one zone to the east adds one hour to the time. Moving one zone to the west takes away one hour from the time.

Online Maps

Today, there are thousands of maps that are free to explore and use. The Internet has several mapping web sites where you can simply enter a place name or a zip code. The map of your chosen area will come onto the screen. You can then zoom in or out and move the map to new areas.

You can also search for certain things, such as movie theaters. The map can show your area with all the movie theaters marked on it. Online maps can show huge amounts of useful information like this.

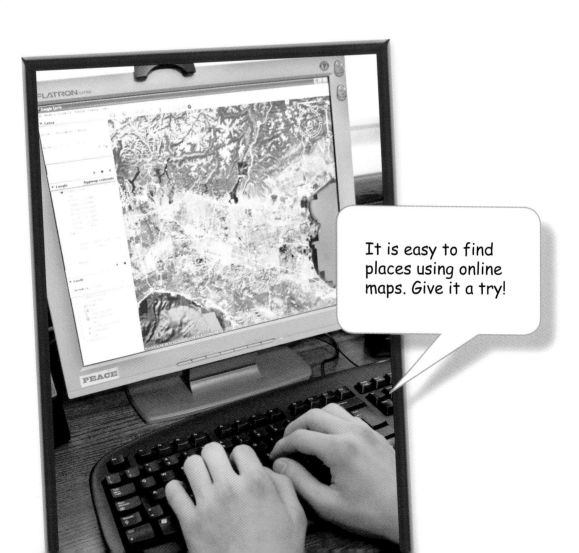

It is easy to find places using online maps. Give it a try!

Planning journeys

Online maps make it really easy to plan journeys. They can figure out the best route and tell you the time you will need to travel. They can show this information on the map, and they also usually list instructions, such as "turn left on Central Street."

GPS DEVICES

Once you are traveling, **GPS** (global positioning system) technology can help prevent you from getting lost! **Satellites** can send signals to cars and cell phones with GPS technology. These can then figure out where you are on their maps and can direct you to where you need to go.

Changing Maps

Some **digital maps** show changing information. They are very useful for people like fishers. Fishing boats can send out **sonar signals** to help locate fish. The digital maps show where the fish are. The maps are always updating and changing as the fish swim around.

Fishers use sonar signals to help them locate fish.

WATCHING THE WEATHER

Digital weather maps can also show changing information. Many people out walking in mountainous areas need up-to-date weather maps to make sure that they do not get caught in bad storms.

High-tech farming

Some farmers use digital maps to help them. Many modern tractors are fitted with GPS devices. These can guide the tractors up and down fields in perfectly straight lines. Before, farmers had to concentrate all the time to make sure they were plowing in straight lines. Now, they can take their hands off the wheel and let the GPS do the steering! The maps update and change as the tractor moves, keeping it on track.

This farmer uses GPS technology in her tractor.

Strange Maps

Some maps show information by changing the shape and size of the land! The size of an area of land is changed depending on the statistic for that area. A map of the world could show the population of each country in this way. A country with a large population, such as China, would be shown as a huge area. Maps that show information in this way are called **cartograms**.

Compare this map with a standard world map. Australia has a small population, so it is much smaller on this map.

Squeezed and stretched

Many transit maps, such as train maps, are made much simpler than in real life. Railroad lines are straightened. Stations are spaced out more evenly. This makes the maps easier to read and understand. They only show the information you need—for example, which railroad lines connect together and which stations they stop at. You do not really need to know the exact distances.

THE LONDON UNDERGROUND MAP

In 1933, a new map of the London Underground was made. People did not like the map at first because it was not geographically correct. However, many transit maps around the world are now based on it.

Making Statistical Maps

Making statistical maps is a bit different from making other types of maps. Usually you will use a "base map" of an area that shows only the borders between countries or regions. The rest of the map is left blank for you to fill in with the information you are interested in.

You can use shades of color, different colors, dots, symbols, or lines to show information on a map. It depends on the information you want to show.

Geographical information systems

A **geographical information system**, or GIS, is a computer system that holds lots of different information. All of the information is linked to a place on a map. The information could be about anything—weather, soil type, population, traffic, or buildings—as long as it is linked to a place.

When using a GIS, people first need to decide what information they are interested in. Then they can get the computer to plot that information on a map. There might be only one layer of information or lots of different layers! A GIS can compare the information in different layers.

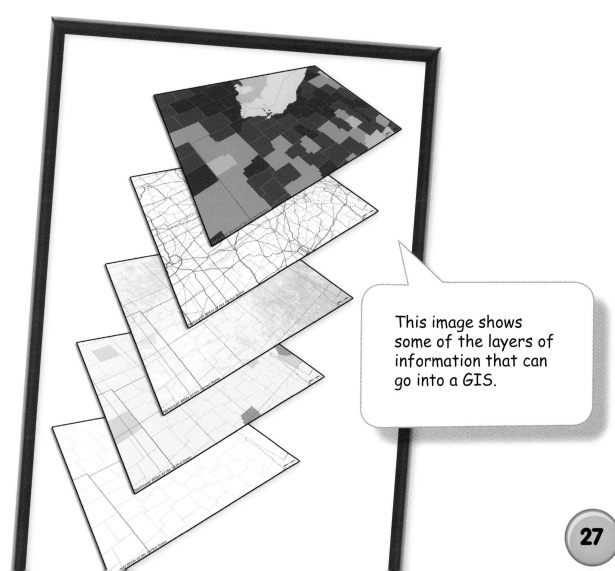

This image shows some of the layers of information that can go into a GIS.

Get Mapping!

Why not try making your own geographical information system? Your classmates or teacher can help you find the information you need.

1) First, make a blank "base map" of your school. Your school office may already have something like this. Make sure it shows all the classrooms.

2) Now use tracing paper to make layers of information for your GIS. Each layer could show a different type of information, for example:

- number of students in each classroom
- average age of students in each classroom
- average height of students in each classroom
- dots for every five students, to show where people go at recess.

3) For each layer, decide which type of map would be best. Do you want to use shades of color? Do you want to make a dot map? If you want to use shades of color, decide which colors would be best.

4) Finally, you can insert all the layers into a file with the base map at the bottom. You now have your own GIS!

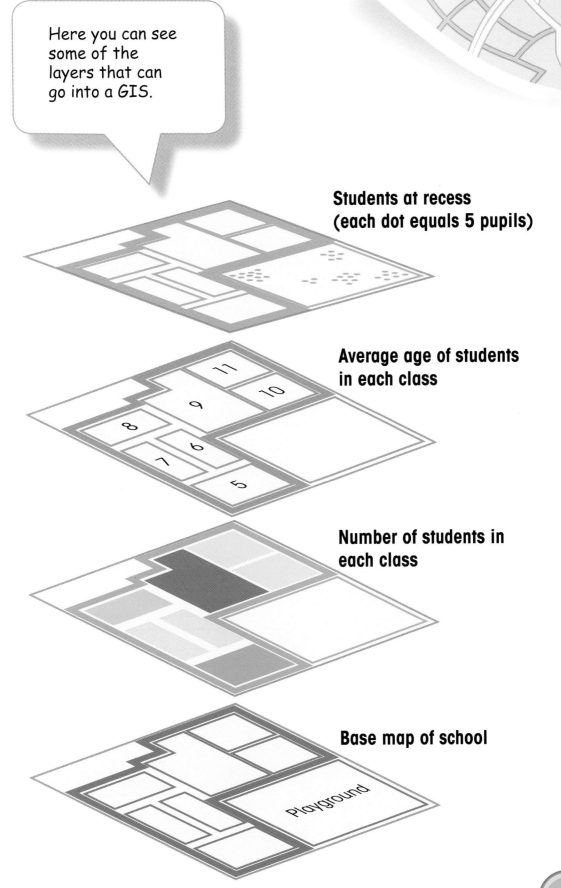

Here you can see some of the layers that can go into a GIS.

Students at recess (each dot equals 5 pupils)

Average age of students in each class

Number of students in each class

Base map of school

Playground

Glossary

aerial photograph photograph taken from high above Earth's surface, usually from an airplane

border imaginary line that separates different countries or different regions inside a country

cartogram map that changes the size and shape of countries as a way of showing information about each country

digital map map that is shown on a screen such as a computer or a cell phone

flow line line on a map that can show the movement of something

geographical information system computer system with lots of different layers of information

GPS (global positioning system) system that uses signals from satellites to find your exact location and to direct you to another location

isoline line joining points that are equal in some way

key list of symbols and an explanation of what each one represents

natural feature something on Earth's surface that has been created by nature—for example, a mountain

North Pole world's northernmost tip

ocean current huge body of seawater that flows in the same direction; it can be warm or cold

percentage amount of something that is represented as a portion of 100 percent

resource something of value to humans that Earth can provide

satellite spacecraft that travels around Earth and gathers or sends back information

satellite image picture, like a photograph, that a satellite can take of Earth from space

solar power station building that captures energy from the Sun's rays and turns it into electricity

sonar signal sonar is short for "sound navigation and ranging"; a sonar signal is a sound signal that is used to find objects underwater

South Pole world's southernmost tip

symbol object or a picture that represents something

Find Out More

There is a whole world of maps and mapping waiting to be discovered! Begin by looking at these books and web sites.

Books

Hennessey, B. G., and Peter Joyce. *The Once Upon a Time Map Book*. Somerville, Mass.: Candlewick, 2010.

Henzel, Cynthia Kennedy. *Reading Maps* (On the Map). Edina, Minn.: ABDO, 2008.

Johnson, Jinny. *Maps and Mapping* (Inside Access). Boston: Kingfisher, 2007.

Torpie, Kate. *Reading Maps* (All Over the Map). New York: Crabtree, 2008.

Web sites

earthpulse.nationalgeographic.com/earthpulse/earthpulse-map
On this web site, you can see a lot of different geographical information on a world map. Simply click on the layer of information you are interested in, in the list on the left, and the map will show the information.

maps.google.com
Here you can find maps of any area in the world. You can zoom in and out, and you can view land from the ground.

www.nationalatlas.gov
This U.S. government web site offers many different kinds of maps of the United States, such as maps that show different types of land, weather, and the number of people living in an area.

www.nationalgeographic.com/kids-world-atlas/maps.html
This National Geographic page is full of links to information about maps. The resources listed here will help you create your own maps, find maps for school reports, zoom in on different parts of the world, and much more!

Index